Denver MEMORIES

THE EARLY YEARS · A PICTORIAL HISTORY

presented by

THE DENVER POST

ACKNOWLEDGMENTS

The Denver Post is pleased to present *Denver Memories: The Early Years*. It must be noted, however, that this unique pictorial history book would not have been possible without the generous contributions made by many people from virtually every corner of our community.

We are indebted, first of all, to those early area residents who captured their time—our history—in photographs, and provided a glimpse into their lives.

Secondly, all area residents are indebted to the many individuals who are committed to preserving our history in various libraries, historical societies, archives and personal collections throughout our community.

The following organizations have contributed greatly to this project:
Black American West Museum
Colorado Railroad Museum
Colorado State Archives
Denver Fire Fighters Museum
Denver Police Museum
Denver Post Archives
Molly Brown House Museum
National Western Stock Show
The Denver Athletic Club
The Denver Public Library, Western History Collection
The Forney Museum of Transportation
The Telecommunications History Group, Inc.
Wings over the Rockies Air and Space Museum

Writer and copy editor: Dana Plewka, The Denver Post
Project manager and editor: Dana Plewka, The Denver Post

Special thanks to: Steve Johansson, The Denver Post; and John Sunderland, retired Denver Post photo editor

FOREWORD

As *The Denver Post* celebrates its 125th year, we are pleased to publish this limited-edition book documenting the visual history of the Denver area from the early 1800s to 1939.

While some photos are from *The Denver Post* archives and from our partnering organizations, we are most excited to share photos submitted by our readers. Many of these photos come from old photo albums handed down from generation to generation. Most of those photos have never before been in public view.

We have captured images of the early days of Denver's settlement and growth; commerce and culture; and what life was like for our settlers. The faces of the people tell a deeper story of boom and bust, struggle and celebration.

This book includes photos representing events that are a significant part of our history such as the end of World War I and the Great Depression. Included are images that celebrate the fashion of the day, sports and theater pastimes. And lest we forget, we acknowledge women's and minorities' many contributions to our great city.

Some buildings in these photos still stand and are easily recognized, while so many others were lost in Denver's hunger for space to grow for the future generations.

We thank all those who provided photos for this book, the organizations and the individuals who have preserved our past. We hope this timeless record of Denver's history will educate and enlighten the next generations about this beautiful place we call home.

Please enjoy this book, hopefully the first of a multiyear series.

Mac Tully
CEO and Publisher
The Denver Post

TABLE OF CONTENTS

OPPOSITE: Construction of the Tramway Building, March 27, 1911. COURTESY FORNEY MUSEUM OF TRANSPORTATION

CHAPTER ONE

VIEWS AND STREET SCENES

This view of a vibrant Sixteenth Street business center says so much about our city. Taken in 1938, it illustrates Denver's crossroads of early motorized vehicles driving across tramway rails; a bustling economy on the cusp of the Great Depression and a society that supported numerous cultural and entertainment businesses. All capped with the Daniels and Fisher tower soaring in the distance.

But it wasn't always that way. Denver's streets in the late 1800s consisted of dirt and mud with wooden sidewalks. It wasn't very easy to get to the Central Business District or area churches on horse-drawn carriages.

The city still carries the name of the Wyoming Territory governor, James W. Denver, who was first petitioned to establish our city. Downtown streets still carry the names of many of our city founders: Wynkoop, Blake, Larimer, Lawrence, Curtis, and Welton.

Architecture tells the story about how cities evolve. We can learn a lot about political and cultural priorities based on choices made in business, religious, cultural, and civic spaces throughout our history.

What is striking about these images is how open and wide our city looked. As you flip through the pages, you'll see streets that could accommodate carriages, automobiles and trolleys all at the same time. And while you won't see much space between the buildings, you also won't see many buildings taller than four stories.

And notice the people walking—all before Sixteenth Street was converted to a pedestrian mall in 1982.

OPPOSITE: The main business street of Denver (Sixteenth Street) looking north, circa 1938. COURTESY DENVER PUBLIC LIBRARY, WESTERN HISTORY COLLECTION, ID# X-23375

ABOVE: Panorama believed to be taken from the tower of Central Presbyterian Church at East Seventeenth Avenue and Sherman Street, 1892.
COURTESY DENVER PUBLIC LIBRARY, WESTERN HISTORY COLLECTION, ID# DPL-88

RIGHT: Rooftop view of Larimer Street showing a busy business district, 1875. City Hall can be seen in the background. COURTESY DENVER PUBLIC LIBRARY, WESTERN HISTORY COLLECTION, ID# X-17643

FAR RIGHT: Fifteenth Street with a horsecar in the foreground, circa 1875. The Lawrence Street fire tower is visible in the distance.
COURTESY DENVER PUBLIC LIBRARY, WESTERN HISTORY COLLECTION, ID# X-23648

OPPOSITE: Denver Tramway Company Seventeenth Avenue trolleys number 45 and 42 on Sixteenth Avenue at the corner of Champa Street, circa 1905.
COURTESY FORNEY MUSEUM OF TRANSPORTATION

ABOVE: Larimer Street from across Cherry Creek in the Central Business District of Denver, circa 1885. The large stone building at left is City Hall.
COURTESY DENVER PUBLIC LIBRARY, WESTERN HISTORY COLLECTION, ID# Z-11788

ABOVE LEFT: Lawrence Street near the intersection of Sixteenth Street, circa 1885.
COURTESY DENVER PUBLIC LIBRARY, WESTERN HISTORY COLLECTION, ID# X-22728

LEFT: Aerial view of Denver in 1883, including Nineteenth and Welton Streets. The buildings in the distance include: Union Station, the Tabor Block with a square corner tower, the Windsor Hotel, Arapahoe School, and the First Presbyterian Church.
COURTESY DENVER PUBLIC LIBRARY, WESTERN HISTORY COLLECTION, WHJ-10448

OPPOSITE: Looking up Seventeenth Street, through the Welcome Arch, from Union Depot, circa 1908.
COURTESY LIBRARY OF CONGRESS, PRINTS & PHOTOGRAPHS DIVISION, DETROIT PUBLISHING COMPANY COLLECTION

ABOVE: Denver Tramway Company trolley number 152 heading south past houses on Bannock Street, circa 1905. The Colorado General Hospital smokestack is in the background. COURTESY FORNEY MUSEUM OF TRANSPORTATION

ABOVE RIGHT: A view of Denver in the late 1800s, including The Wentworth, a hotel owned and operated by A. H. Estes. COURTESY NEVA MURPHY

RIGHT: Looking down a brick-paved Wynkoop Street to Union Station, rebuilt after the 1894 fire, circa 1900. COURTESY DENVER PUBLIC LIBRARY, WESTERN HISTORY COLLECTION, ID# MCC-284

LEFT: Broadway looking north from Seventeenth Street, circa 1905. Hotel Metropole, opened in 1891 by William H. Bush, later became part of Cosmopolitan Hotel. In the background on the right is Trinity Methodist Church. COURTESY DENVER PUBLIC LIBRARY, WESTERN HISTORY COLLECTION, ID# MCC-1175

BELOW LEFT: Street scene after the December 1913 blizzard. COURTESY BETTY BARTLETT

BELOW: Sidewalk along Sixteenth Street with elaborate electric street lights, circa 1906. Identifiable businesses include Sorosis Shoe store (626 Sixteenth), Singer Sewing Machine Company salesroom (628 Sixteenth), and A. T. Lewis and Son (810–818 Sixteenth). COURTESY DENVER PUBLIC LIBRARY, WESTERN HISTORY COLLECTION, ID# MCC-634

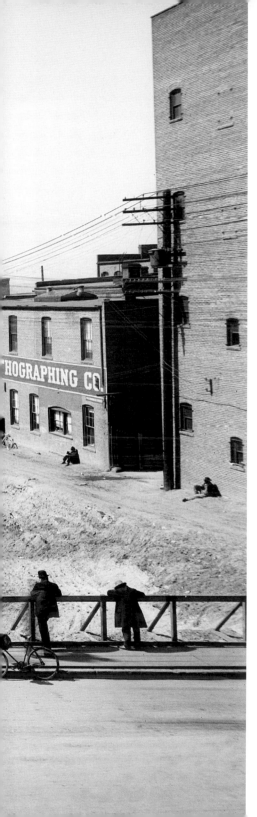

ABOVE: Sixteenth and California Streets, circa 1915. The Daniels and Fisher clock tower on Arapahoe Street is in the background.

COURTESY ANNETTE COHEN

OPPOSITE: A construction site on Arapahoe Street between Thirteenth and Fourteenth Streets draws onlookers, May 1, 1910.

COURTESY FORNEY MUSEUM OF TRANSPORTATION

ABOVE RIGHT: Panoramic view of Denver from the dome of the State Capitol Building, 1928. Landmarks include Arapahoe County Courthouse, Mountain States Bell Telephone and Telegraph Building, the Republic Building, Majestic and Metropolitan Buildings, and the Daniels & Fishers clock tower.

COURTESY DENVER PUBLIC LIBRARY, WESTERN HISTORY COLLECTION, ID# X-29106

BELOW RIGHT: The intersection of Eighteenth and Larimer Streets in downtown Denver, circa 1925.

COURTESY DENVER PUBLIC LIBRARY, WESTERN HISTORY COLLECTION, X-23473

BELOW: Fifteenth Street with Mining Exchange Building and Denver Gas and Electric Light Company (DG&E) Building, circa 1915.

COURTESY DENVER PUBLIC LIBRARY, WESTERN HISTORY COLLECTION, ID# MCC-3847

ABOVE: The new Civic Center Park not long after it was completed in 1919. Visible here is the 1910 "Old Main" building of the Denver Public Library, one of the Carnegie Libraries, on the right at Colfax and Bannock. The Greek Theater (left) and Voorhies Memorial (far right) were gifts to the city from its wealthy residents. COURTESY EUGENE X. TEPPER

LEFT: Curtis Street, looking toward Eighteenth Street from Sixteenth Street, circa 1936. COURTESY SALLIE C. LEWIS

CHAPTER TWO

TRANSPORTATION

First they came on horseback and then in wagon trains and carriages. A watering hole at Colfax and Broadway enticed travelers to stop for a while; and some stayed on.

Horse-drawn trolleys and even some forms of "cart pooling" made it easier to get around the quickly expanding city.

Bicycles and motorcycles weren't only for transportation; they were also often part of clubs and social gatherings.

Railroads opened the West for migrations from the East, and Union Station was a welcome sight for many. Denver Tramway's electric trolleys and the development of automobiles allowed the city to sprawl. Often, many of these modes of transportation co-existed on the same city streets simultaneously.

By the early 1900s, Denver boasted of having multiple automobile dealerships to accommodate the needs of people in the entire region.

With a growing population and multiple modes of transportation came the urgency for renewed investment in infrastructure of paved roads, bridges, rail tracks, and more—which, in turn, spurred more migration to Denver.

Amelia Earhart and Charles Lindbergh included Denver in their US air tours, thrilling thousands of onlookers.

OPPOSITE: Travelers in the back of an observation car on track one at Denver Union Station ready to start a journey south towards Pueblo, circa 1925.
COURTESY COLORADO RAILROAD MUSEUM

ABOVE: Clear Creek Avenue horse-drawn trolley, late 1800s.
COURTESY COLORADO RAILROAD MUSEUM

ABOVE RIGHT: Ruins of the original Denver Union Station, built in 1881, burned on March 18, 1894, when a fire ignited the electrical system in the ladies' restroom.
COURTESY DENVER PUBLIC LIBRARY, WESTERN HISTORY COLLECTION, ID# X-25203

RIGHT: Street cars and horse-drawn wagons and carriages on a busy Seventeenth Street as seen from the train depot in the late 1800s. The space in the center of this view would soon be occupied by the famous Welcome Arch.
COURTESY COLORADO RAILROAD MUSEUM

LEFT: The Cribb family at City Park in August of 1897 as they started their attempt to ride Victor bicycles to St. Louis to claim a prize of $1,000 if the trip was completed in ten days or less. A large crowd of 500 people sent them off on their journey after a newspaper article ran the day before. Unfortunately, the family gave up after four treacherous days of travel. From left: Tryphena Violette Cribb, Oliver Cromwell Cribb, Eugenie Louise Drescher Cribb, Olive Leslie Cribb (Headstrom). The family is in front of a statue that was created for the 1893 Chicago World's Fair and given to Denver when the fair was dismantled. The statue did not weather the outside display in Denver and no longer exists. The Cribb family moved to Denver for only one year after losing everything in the St. Louis tornado of 1896. After their year in Denver the family moved back to St. Louis and then Des Moines, Iowa. Leslie Cribb Headstrom moved back to Denver and spent her final years here. COURTESY RICHARD HEADSTROM

BELOW LEFT: Men and bicycles in front of G. E. Hannan bicycle store, circa 1895. COURTESY DENVER PUBLIC LIBRARY, WESTERN HISTORY COLLECTION, ID# X-18215

BELOW: Early automobiles in front of Colorado Winton Motor Carriage Company and the Bicycle Supply Company at the corner of Eighteenth and Stout Streets, circa 1902. COURTESY DENVER PUBLIC LIBRARY, WESTERN HISTORY COLLECTION, ID# C-2

ABOVE LEFT: John Bogue, (conductor, driver, and lessee) leans out the front of the Cherrelyn horsecar with the horse on the back platform, circa 1903. The horse pulled the car to Englewood then coasted back down the hill, getting a much-needed rest.
COURTESY FRED TEAL

BELOW LEFT: John Anderson Transfer and Storage wagon in front of the Denver Mint in the early 1900s.
COURTESY DENVER PUBLIC LIBRARY, WESTERN HISTORY COLLECTION, ID# DENVER MINT / HARRY M. RHOADS

OPPOSITE: Livery stable in the Auraria Neighborhood, 1905, located on the banks of Cherry Creek in the heart of downtown Denver. Auraria is Denver's oldest neighborhood, which predates the city's establishment in 1861.
COURTESY JIM MCNALLY

ABOVE: Denver Tramway Company trolleys, number 56 and number 73, at the intersection of Thirty-Second Avenue and Zuni Street, circa 1902. COURTESY FORNEY MUSEUM OF TRANSPORTATION

RIGHT: The Nineteenth Avenue streetcar at Lakeside, early 1900s. COURTESY RAYMOND CARREKER

OPPOSITE: Denver Tramway Company sightseeing car number 112 in front of the Brown Palace Hotel on Seventeenth Street, circa 1905. COURTESY FORNEY MUSEUM OF TRANSPORTATION

ABOVE: Denver Tramway Company's early electric car and trailer at Sixteenth and Curtis Streets, circa 1906. COURTESY COLORADO RAILROAD MUSEUM

ABOVE LEFT: Denver Tramway Company machine shop and armature room, circa 1905. COURTESY FORNEY MUSEUM OF TRANSPORTATION

LEFT: The first shipment of Cadillacs received in Denver is lined up in front of the Saint James Hotel, Fifteenth and Curtis Streets, circa 1905. COURTESY DENVER PUBLIC LIBRARY, WESTERN HISTORY COLLECTION, ID# RH-680

OPPOSITE: T. J. O'Donnell and friends in a Thomas Flyer at the 1500 block of Race Street, circa 1910. The vehicle was manufactured in Buffalo, New York. COURTESY CANTON O'DONNELL

ABOVE: Workers sit on Denver and Rio Grande Railroad engine number 1001 at Union Station, circa 1905.

COURTESY DENVER PUBLIC LIBRARY, WESTERN HISTORY COLLECTION, ID# Z-5472

ABOVE RIGHT: "Carpooling" in 1907. This wagon provided transportation to Denver near Third Avenue and Downing Street, to catch a streetcar. Sitting in the back are Maude Crosby and her husband, State Senator James Crosby.

COURTESY MELISSA ADAMS

RIGHT: In the early 1900s, a regular Union Depot-Central Loop shuttle route provided fast connections to all parts of Denver for arriving rail passengers.

COURTESY COLORADO RAILROAD MUSEUM

LEFT: Barn and dairy delivery wagons belonging to John Mayberry, circa 1900. John's father, Samuel Mayberry, started the dairy in 1876 after moving his family to Colorado from Ontario, Canada. John married Miss Viola Whitehead on October 2, 1889, and the couple had 10 children: Ralph; Homer; Vassie, who married Otto Anger; Evan, who married Ebba Johnson; Marie; Agnes; Lulu; Richard; Robert; Zoe. John is the grandfather of Gladys Anger Capp, the photo donor's mother. COURTESY GINGER ZOTT

BELOW LEFT: Agnes Donovan Kitt (right), her four-month-old son, Fred T. Kitt (on her lap), and her sister, Cecelia Donovan (at wheel), August 9, 1910. Photo probably was posed on the ground in Louis Paulhan's Farman bi-plane, restored after Denver's first flights on February 4, 1910, and used as photographer's prop. An unknown scene was used as a backdrop. Paulhan brought heavier-than-air aviation to Denver when he thrilled onlookers with his Farman biplane at the Overland Park racetrack. COURTESY DENNIS TANGNEY

BELOW: French aviator Louis Paulhan (in scarf) and two other men inspect a Gnome engine attached to the propeller of a Farman airplane at Overland Park, February 1910. Paulhan is credited with the first heavier-than-air flight in Denver, February 4, 1910. COURTESY DENVER PUBLIC LIBRARY, WESTERN HISTORY COLLECTION, ID# RH-703

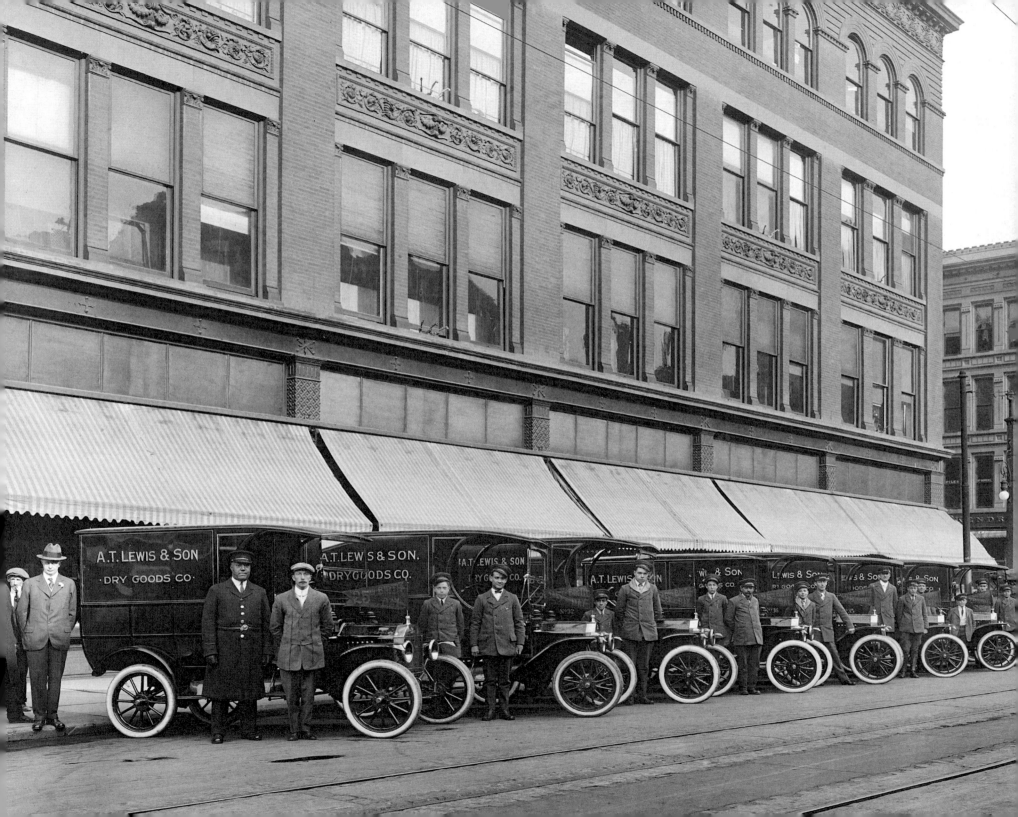

ABOVE LEFT: Harry Gutheil on an Indian motorcycle, circa 1912.
COURTESY DARCIE MEIERBACHTOL

BELOW LEFT: Carl Stapper (left) and friend with bikes at 2516 Woodbury Court, circa 1910.
COURTESY ELLIE MCNEILL

OPPOSITE: A fleet of new 1915 Model-T delivery trucks in front of A. T. Lewis & Sons Department Store at Sixteenth and Stout Streets.
COURTESY KATHY BUSCH

ABOVE: Spectators looking at an accident scene between a coal truck and a streetcar, circa 1920. COURTESY DENVER PUBLIC LIBRARY, WESTERN HISTORY COLLECTION, ID# RH-405

RIGHT: Albert Perras worked as a conductor for the Denver and Rio Grande Railroad, 1924. COURTESY CHARLES T. LANKFORD

OPPOSITE: Denver Tramway trolley cars 116, 197 and 171 overturned on East Colfax Avenue during the Denver streetcar strike the first week of August 1920. During the strike, several people were killed and injured. On August 6, a conference was held between state and city authorities with Governor Shoup requesting federal troops be sent to Denver. Troops were sent from Fort Logan at 1:30 a.m. the following morning, and martial law was declared. Rioting ceased and martial law ended on September 8. A limited number of soldiers stayed behind to help Denver police through the end of the month. In the background, the Cathedral Basilica of the Immaculate Conception is the cathedral of the Archdiocese of Denver of the Roman Catholic Church. It is located at the corner of Logan Street and Colfax Avenue in the North Capitol Hill neighborhood of central Denver. COURTESY FRED TEAL

ABOVE: A. L. Smith (left), the grandfather of Pat Smith Sandstedt, was a trolley car conductor for the Denver Tramway, circa 1915. COURTESY PAT SMITH SANDSTEDT

ABOVE LEFT: Union Station in the early 1900s.
COURTESY COLORADO RAILROAD MUSEUM

LEFT: Elizabeth Bacarri in her new Packard with chains on the rear wheels for driving in the snow, circa 1920.
COURTESY STEVE KNIGHT

OPPOSITE: Denver & Rio Grande Western (D&RGW) locomotive Class L-132, No. 3613, pictured here on a hoist in the Burnham Shops was built in 1930 and scrapped in May, 1956. COURTESY COLORADO RAILROAD MUSEUM

ABOVE: Walter Highley, pilot, businessman, and educator, by a Waco cabin airplane in Denver with Les Bowman and Edna McLaughlin, circa 1932.

COURTESY DENVER PUBLIC LIBRARY, WESTERN HISTORY COLLECTION, ID# X-21965

ABOVE RIGHT: Pioneer aviator Amelia Earhart landed her Autogiro helicopter-like plane at the Denver Municipal Airport on one of her many cross-country excursions in June 1931. The transcontinental flight was sponsored by Beech-Nut chewing gum. She visited Denver three times between 1931 and 1936. Photo was taken by William J. Schneider, the photo donor's father, at the Denver Municipal Airport when he was 14 years old.

COURTESY MARY SCHNEIDER SUCHEY

RIGHT: Amelia Earhart and Frederick G. Bonfils, editor and publisher of *The Denver Post*, with the Pitcairn PCA-2 Autogiro, June 1931. Earhart became the first woman to fly an autogiro and had less than an hour of training.

COURTESY DENVER PUBLIC LIBRARY, WESTERN HISTORY COLLECTION, ID# RH-173

ABOVE: Albert Robson was one of the first to fly his own plane in Denver, 1929. COURTESY CHARLES T. LANKFORD

LEFT: Denver Municipal Airport (later became Stapleton Airport in 1944) during development, 1927. COURTESY ROBERT BEABOUT

ABOVE: Chicago, Burlington & Quincy Railroad locomotive shop, September 12, 1926.
COURTESY DENVER PUBLIC LIBRARY, WESTERN HISTORY COLLECTION, ID# OTTO C. PERRY PHOTO, OP-4884

LEFT: A bus operated by Union Pacific Stages, a subsidiary of Union Pacific Railroad, July 1930. The company purchased the routes of Pickwick-Greyhound Lines between Denver and Salt Lake City, and between Salt Lake City and Los Angeles. Pickwick-Greyhound operated in cooperation with Greyhound as a separate company until it went bankrupt during the Depression.
COURTESY COLORADO RAILROAD MUSEUM

OPPOSITE: Union Pacific employees from the Twenty-Third Street coach yard greet the westbound run of the City of Denver behind the M-10005 engine on the final curve of its 1,000-mile overnight trip from the shore of Lake Michigan, June 1936.
COURTESY COLORADO RAILROAD MUSEUM

ABOVE: Denver Tramway car passing through high water by the Montgomery Ward building at South Broadway and Virginia Avenue during the Cherry Creek flood of 1933.
COURTESY COLORADO RAILROAD MUSEUM

RIGHT: William Joseph Gallagher in engine No. 303, most likely at the Moffat Depot at Fifteenth and Bassett Streets, circa 1939. No. 303 was a Denver & Salt Lake Class 34, 4-6-0 built by Schenectady in July of 1910 and dismantled July of 1948. Gallagher later worked for the Rio Grande Railroad. COURTESY DENNIS GALLAGHER

OPPOSITE: Cab drivers parked in front of the state capitol building in the 1940s. "Junior" Juniel, who drove Dr. Justina Ford to her calls, is second from the right.
COURTESY BLACK AMERICAN WEST MUSEUM, PAUL W. STEWART COLLECTION

CHAPTER THREE

SCHOOLS AND EDUCATION

The earliest families to arrive in Denver had only themselves to depend on for schooling. Settlers taught their children at home or local churches.

St. Mary's Academy at Fourteenth and California Streets was Denver's first girls' school. Loretto Heights Academy built an elementary and secondary school in 1890.

No chapter about education would be complete without mention of Emily Griffith, who pioneered Denver public education and founded the school that still carries her name.

Griffith believed everyone deserved an education, regardless of age, race, gender, or background. Such thinking was very forward for that time.

Whether class sizes were large or small, urban or rural, they all played a significant role in bringing families together as part of a community. The establishment of the University of Denver in 1864 also added higher education, and college sports to the Rocky Mountain Region.

OPPOSITE: Teller School graduation band from the sixth grade, January 1931. COURTESY JULIA ROMEO HAEN

ABOVE: St. Mary's Academy faculty from Fourteenth and California Streets, July 1886. Sisters of Loretto: Sister M. Paschal, Sister Dolorine Powers, Sister Alathea, Sister Bartholomew, Sister Menadora, Sister Romana, Sister Columba. The girls in white are M. Cody and B. Finley.

COURTESY LORETTO HERITAGE CENTER. PHOTO BY E.N. CLEMENTS

ABOVE RIGHT: Cadets in uniforms with rifles in front of Denver High School (East Side High School), circa 1894. COURTESY DENVER PUBLIC LIBRARY, WESTERN HISTORY COLLECTION, ID# X-19792

RIGHT: Construction of the Administration building for Loretto Heights Academy, an elementary and secondary school for girls, 1890. Originally called Tower Hall, this was the first building on campus. F. E. Edbrooke was the architect.

COURTESY MARY NELLE GAGE, SL/SISTERS OF LORETTO

LEFT: Denver High School football team of 1897.
COURTESY DENVER PUBLIC LIBRARY, WESTERN HISTORY COLLECTION, ID# Z-2255

BELOW LEFT: Gilpin School football champions of 1894 in front of the school at Twenty-Ninth and Stout Streets in the Five Points neighborhood of Denver. COURTESY DENVER PUBLIC LIBRARY, WESTERN HISTORY COLLECTION, ID# X-28415

BELOW: Manual Training High School Bowling Club team, 1901. Bowling was just coming into existence at this time with professional-looking uniforms. It is believed M & O was a cigar company.
COURTESY JIM MCNALLY

ABOVE: Players and the coach of the girls' basketball team on the steps of Manual Training High School at Twenty-Seventh and Franklin Streets in the Whittier neighborhood, circa 1905. COURTESY DENVER PUBLIC LIBRARY, WESTERN HISTORY COLLECTION, ID# X-28487

LEFT: A group of student nurses at the entrance of Denver Homeopathic Hospital and Medical College at Park Avenue and Humboldt Street in the City Park West neighborhood of Denver, circa 1905. COURTESY DENVER PUBLIC LIBRARY, WESTERN HISTORY COLLECTION, ID# X-28598

OPPOSITE: The 1908 closing exercises at St. Mary's Academy honored eighth-grade girls in the junior department with beautiful scrolls similar to the diplomas they would receive four years later. COURTESY REGINA DREY/ST. MARY'S ACADEMY

ABOVE: The Haish Building, home of the University of Denver Law School, Fourteenth and Arapahoe Streets, circa 1900. The University of Denver College of Law opened its doors in 1892, and in September 2004, became the Sturm College of Law. COURTESY UNIVERSITY OF DENVER STURM COLLEGE OF LAW

ABOVE RIGHT: Girls wood carving class at Manual Training High School, circa 1908. Manual Training High School was located in the Whittier neighborhood of Denver. COURTESY DENVER PUBLIC LIBRARY, WESTERN HISTORY COLLECTION, ID# X-28473

RIGHT: East High School championship baseball team of 1903. Front row, from left: Donald Reid, William Davis, Edward Shedd. Middle row: Alfred Goudy, Randolph Ballinger, Herbert Dudley (Captain), Joe Ashton, Albert Reid. Back row: Scott Nance, Harry Cohen, Montgomery Smith, Bertram Siddons, Arthur Copeland (Manager). COURTESY DENVER PUBLIC LIBRARY, WESTERN HISTORY COLLECTION, ID# Z-3615

OPPOSITE: Opportunity School welding class, circa 1910.
COURTESY DENVER PUBLIC LIBRARY, WESTERN HISTORY COLLECTION,
ID# DENVER EDUCATION-EMILY GRIFFITH OPPORTUNITY SCHOOL / ACETYLENE WELDING CLASS

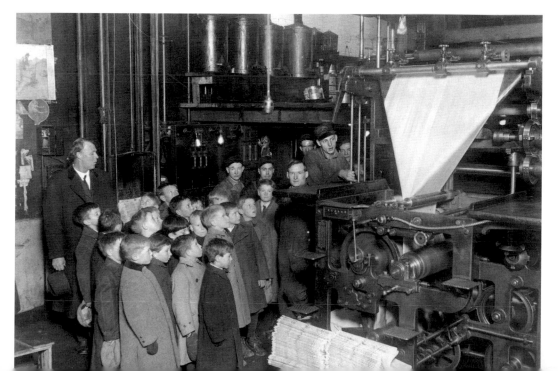

ABOVE: North Denver High School, 2960 North Speer Boulevard, shortly after it was completed in 1911. The building was designed by architect David W. Dryden. COURTESY DENVER PUBLIC LIBRARY, WESTERN HISTORY COLLECTION, ID# MCC-1613

LEFT: Students and their teacher from Clayton College for Boys get a tour of the pressroom at the Denver Post printing plant in 1913.
COURTESY DENVER PUBLIC LIBRARY, WESTERN HISTORY COLLECTION, ID# X-23303

OPPOSITE: Byers Public School, 104 West Byers Place, 1914. Jessie Mae Smith is in the second row, fourth from left. Also included in photo: Blanch Fairies, Creta Jackson, Alma Green, Mrs. Craig (teacher), Bessie Richards, Ethel Lamb, Maisie Crabb, Iriene Parmely, Jessie Smith, Ruth Dickerson, Marg Fuller, Irma Grunawalt, Miss McKlure, Miles Hubbard, Dwight Frie, Earnest Su, Robert Bradfield, George Shnittz, Cedric Sone.
COURTESY ROBERT GRAEBER

RIGHT: Elmwood School class of 1916. COURTESY CHARLENE PORTER

BELOW RIGHT: Baseball team from Sacred Heart High school (now Regis University), circa 1917. Second row, second from left is Fred O. Burke. COURTESY ROSEMARY BURKE

OPPOSITE: Students being picked up by a Denver Public Schools bus on a cold winter day in the Montclair Neighborhood, 1920. COURTESY JIM MCNALLY

ABOVE: Emily Griffith, a pioneer in Denver public education, came to the city with her family in 1894 at age 26 and began teaching in Denver schools. She became deputy state superintendent of schools in 1904 and served in that position for six years. Griffith also taught night classes for adults. She believed everyone deserved an education regardless of age, race, gender, or background. In 1916, Griffith opened Opportunity School. By the time she retired in 1933, more than 100,000 students had attended her school which was renamed in her honor that same year. COURTESY DENVER PUBLIC LIBRARY, WESTERN HISTORY COLLECTION, ID# DENVER EDUCATION-EMILY GRIFFITH OPPORTUNITY SCHOOL / WOMEN'S AUTO SHOP CLASS

ABOVE LEFT: Corona School's June class of 1919. COURTESY DUDLEY SMITH

LEFT: The eighth-grade graduating class of Valverde Public School, 1919. Ann Harnby, is the girl with the long curls in the front row. She was born in 1906 and lived in Denver all her life. COURTESY CATHY WANSTRATH

OPPOSITE: Emily Griffith Opportunity School women's auto shop class in the 1920s. COURTESY DENVER PUBLIC LIBRARY, WESTERN HISTORY COLLECTION, ID# BIOGRAPHY / GRIFFITH, EMILY

ABOVE: Denver Public School custodians' picnic at Genesee Mountain Park, June 18,1927.

COURTESY FAMILY OF EDWARD E. SAUVÉ

RIGHT: Englewood High School, class of 1924.

COURTESY CHARLES T. LANKFORD

OPPOSITE BOTTOM: Montclair Grade School staff and students in front of the school on East Thirteenth Avenue and Quebec Street, circa 1920. The principal at the time was Miss Charlotte Godsman. COURTESY EUGENE A. BLISH

ABOVE: Children studying at tables in the library at Steele Public School, 320 South Marion Street Parkway, circa 1932. COURTESY DENVER PUBLIC LIBRARY, WESTERN HISTORY COLLECTION, ID# MCC-3802

ABOVE LEFT: Members of the University of Denver "Pioneers" football team and their coaches in 1926. COURTESY DENVER PUBLIC LIBRARY, WESTERN HISTORY COLLECTION, ID# Z-10009

LEFT: Students and teachers at Webster School, West Thirty-Sixth Avenue and Lipan Street in North Denver, circa 1924. Rocco Carabetta is in the second row, second from left. This school combined with Bryant to become Bryant Webster in 1930. COURTESY DOLORES A. LOMBARDI

OPPOSITE: Lafayette School Band in front of the Darrow Music Company at the corner of Fifteenth and Stout Streets during Music Week in 1928. COURTESY LAFAYETTE MINERS MUSEUM

RIGHT: Teller School sixth-grade graduation class, January 1931. COURTESY JULIA ROMEO HAEN

OPPOSITE: Lake Junior High School Spring Regatta at Sloan's Lake Park, circa 1930.
COURTESY DENVER PUBLIC LIBRARY, WESTERN HISTORY COLLECTION, ID# X-27730

BELOW: Lake Junior High School, 1930. The school was built in 1926 and designed by architects Merrill H. and Burnham F. Hoyt.
COURTESY VIRGINIA BRAY

ABOVE: The 1936 Manual Training High School football team known as the Bricklayers. Wearing jersey number 20 is Donald MacMillian. COURTESY JAMES F. ROGERS

LEFT: Regis High School prom attendees in 1937. The photo donor's father, Bill Doyle, is standing seventh from the right. COURTESY DIANA K. DOYLE

OPPOSITE BOTTOM LEFT: Baker Junior High School eighth-grade class in 1938. Annabelle Pardee is one of the students in this class. COURTESY SANDY NEELY

OPPOSITE BOTTOM RIGHT: A group of young people celebrating their graduation from St. Francis De Sales High School, circa 1938. Foster A. Papi is at front right. COURTESY RACHELLA SEELEY

GROCERIES
BRUNO BROS.
MEA
2504. BRUNO BROS. GROCERIES
2506 BRUNO BROS.
2504½
LENOX SOAP
WATER WHITE SOAP
BRUNO BROS
PROVISIONS
BRUNO BROS
GROCERIES
BRUNO BRO'S
MARKET
WATER WHITE SOAP
SOAP
MARKET

CHAPTER FOUR

COMMERCE AND INDUSTRY

From the beginning, there were pioneers with goods and services to sell, and their neighbors were eager to pay for them. Grocery and dry-goods stores, and blacksmith and wagon-repair shops quickly dominated Denver's main streets.

The opportunities were bright for entrepreneurs who had a clever idea and were willing to work long, hard hours. Mom-and-pop stores were truly a family operation with parents and children working side by side to make their business successful.

Sibling-owned businesses such as Epley Brickyard and Perini Brothers Company relied on extended family to bring their goods and services to consumers.

And while many small businesses came and went over the years, some grew into large organizations that had a lasting influence in the area. The Daniels and Fisher retail location in downtown Denver built the clock tower that remains a landmark. The Denver Dry Goods Company was a cornerstone of the retail community from 1879 to 1987. The Guiry Brothers wallpaper and paint company still serves its customers at their current location at Seventeenth and Curtis streets.

The demand for skilled and unskilled employees spurred the need for a more diverse workforce that introduced women and minorities into the job market.

OPPOSITE: Bruno Brothers Groceries and Market at 2504-2506 Central Street (later Highland Gateway Park), circa 1912. Ralph Bruno, proprietor, has his foot on the wheel. Other family members are unidentified. COURTESY PATRICK BRUNO

ABOVE: Operators at the main Colorado Telephone Company Office at 1447 Lawrence Street, one of Denver's first fireproof buildings, circa 1889. COURTESY THE TELECOMMUNICATIONS HISTORY GROUP, INC.

RIGHT: Business block in Denver, including Daniels, Fisher & Co. with their delivery wagons on Larimer Street, circa 1875. COURTESY DENVER PUBLIC LIBRARY, WESTERN HISTORY COLLECTION, ID# X-18607

OPPOSITE: Epley Brickyard storage, 1889. From left: John Epley, Buzz Dolby, Hub Powers, Hooks, Jack Buckley, Monte Epley, Gene Vaughn, Charly Apple, Lou Voice, John Seipp, Harry Martin, Ducky Leonard, George Rice, Paul Eley, Fred Meyers. COURTESY DIANA L. FREDERICK

ABOVE: A. Jones general store, late 1800s. COURTESY RAYMOND CARREKER

OPPOSITE: James Hollingsworth (left), a delivery driver for Daniels & Fisher, circa 1892. The young man seated next to James is likely his son, Frank Hollingsworth. COURTESY SHARON GAYLEY

RIGHT: Walter J. Grund driving a delivery wagon for Mayers Market, circa 1896. Grund, the photo donor's grandfather, was born in Boulder in 1880 and moved to Denver in 1886. The meat market was located at 2532 Lawrence Street. COURTESY ANITA WAGNER

BELOW RIGHT: Employees of the McPhee-McGinnity Manufacturing Company on horse-drawn wagons near the company's warehouse at Twenty-Third and Blake Streets in the Five Points neighborhood of Denver, circa 1890. COURTESY DENVER PUBLIC LIBRARY, WESTERN HISTORY COLLECTION, ID# X-24463

BELOW: Lobby of the American House hotel at Sixteenth and Blake Streets, circa 1890. COURTESY DENVER PUBLIC LIBRARY, WESTERN HISTORY COLLECTION, ID# X-29211

ABOVE: Telephone operators exercise on the roof of the Denver Main Exchange, circa 1900. The company also provided lounges in which the operators could relax during their breaks. COURTESY THE TELECOMMUNICATIONS HISTORY GROUP, INC.

ABOVE LEFT: Grant Painting Company employees, along with owners, in front of the store in downtown Denver, 1900. COURTESY CATHY WANSTRATH

LEFT: The Perini Brothers Store, 1900. The store was a specialty shop in operation from 1875-1927 and managed by William Capella. COURTESY REGINA ALSOP

BOYD BRICK PRESS
PATENTED
CHISHOLM BOYD & WHITE CO
CHICAGO

ABOVE: The O. P. Baur Confectionery Co., circa 1900. The business was established in 1872 and this store was 75 feet wide by 125 feet long. COURTESY DENVER PUBLIC LIBRARY, WESTERN HISTORY COLLECTION, ID# Z-2893

LEFT: Arabel Morton in the doorway of her dry goods and notions store at West Forty-First Avenue and Tejon Street, circa 1905. Arabel married Charles Morton in Baltimore and had three sons. Charles was a captain of a ship but was injured and unable to work on the ship. Arabel had family in Denver, so she came back and opened this notion store while Charles worked as a night watchman. Arabel Morton died in 1936. COURTESY DAVID E. MORTON

OPPOSITE: Paul T. Epley (left) and George M. Rice on either side of the "Special Brick Machine," the first such machine in the state of Colorado, November 1903. The men are at Epley Brickyard. COURTESY ELAINE M. SAFE

RIGHT: Leopold H. Guldman, owner of the Golden Eagle department store, immigrated from Bavaria to the United States in 1879. He opened Golden Eagle Dry Goods Company in Leadville and another one at Cripple Creek before opening a third store at 391 Lawrence Street in Denver. He had a few business partners along the way, Simon M. Wineman and Bernhardt Heller. He was good friends with David May, who founded the May Company stores. In the early 1900s, Guldman purchased the Times Building at Sixteenth and Lawrence Streets expanding his business in the five-story building. Before his death in 1936, Guldman was credited with donating Denver's first Jewish Community Center, the Guldman Center, being one of the founders of both the National Jewish Hospital and the Beth Israel Hospital, and donating generously to a number of other charities. After his death the store closed in connection with the estate. The following year Guldman's son-in-law, Lester Friedman reopened the store. Friedman kept the store going through the Depression and into the early 1940s, however, other business took him to Washington, DC, just before World War II and the Golden Eagle permanently closed in 1941. COURTESY DAVID AND PAM WOLF

FAR RIGHT: The Golden Eagle, a successful department store at Lawrence and Sixteenth Streets, was started by Leopold H. Guldman. The young successful immigrant asked a carpenter to carve a large eagle and paint it gold. The eagle was placed over the store's front door, and the store became known as "The Golden Eagle." COURTESY DAVID AND PAM WOLF

BELOW RIGHT: Boulevard Grocery at 2544 Federal Boulevard, circa 1905. The store was owned by Joseph Scioli. The building later housed Micky Manor Tavern. COURTESY PAULA TOMKO

ABOVE: L. C. Fulenwider and his staff, April 1908. Their offices were in the Equitable Building. L. C. Fulenwider Sr. helped write the Colorado Real Estate License laws in the early 1900s and his grandson, Cal Fulenwider III, continues to hold Colorado Real Estate License number one, which originally belonged to his grandfather. The Fulenwider family has owned L. C. Fulenwider, Inc. for four generations, since its founding in 1904. The Fulenwider Family was inducted into the Colorado Business Hall of Fame in 2016. COURTESY L. C. FULENWIDER, INC.

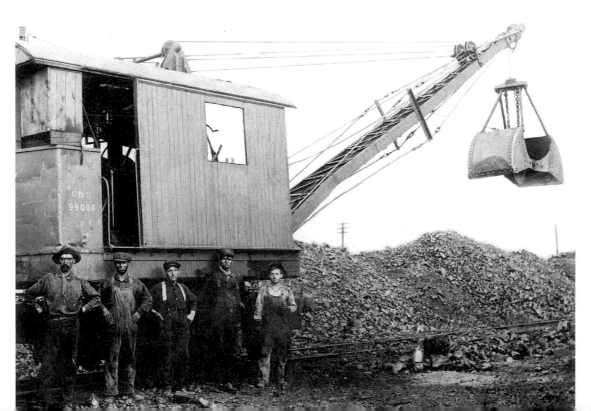

LEFT: Q. J. Gilmore operated the first Black funeral home in Denver, circa 1905. COURTESY BLACK AMERICAN WEST MUSEUM, PAUL W. STEWART COLLECTION

BELOW LEFT: Gerardo Carabetta (far right) with co-workers shoveling coal for the Colorado & Southern Railroad, circa 1905. The C&S coal yard was located on the west side of the present Elitch Gardens. COURTESY FRANK LOMBARDI

OPPOSITE: Athens Confections at 1008-1010 Fifteenth Street in the early 1900s. COURTESY MICHAEL GARYET

ABOVE: Entrance of J. D. Miller's Meat Market at 1035 Fifteenth Street, circa 1912. In preparation for the holidays the market was offering "Turkeys Dressed By Us Today 20 Cents Lb," and "Sugar Cured Half Hams, 10 Cents Lb."
COURTESY DENVER PUBLIC LIBRARY, WESTERN HISTORY COLLECTION, ID# RH-5859

ABOVE RIGHT: Wright Transfer Company truck, circa 1915.
COURTESY BLACK AMERICAN WEST MUSEUM, PAUL W. STEWART COLLECTION

RIGHT: Show grounds and tents at the National Western Stock Show in 1907. COURTESY NATIONAL WESTERN STOCK SHOW

OPPOSITE: National Western stockyard, circa 1918.
COURTESY NATIONAL WESTERN STOCK SHOW

ABOVE: Denver Gas and Electric Light Company employee picnic at Bergen Park, August 14, 1920.
COURTESY BRIAN DUMMER

LEFT: Federal Boulevard Garage, circa 1915. Al Forster was one of 11 children who grew up at the First and Last Chance business on the present-day corner of West Fourth Avenue and Federal Boulevard. In his youth, he owned a bicycle shop adjacent to the First and Last Chance business run by his father, Simon Forster. With the development of the automobile, the business evolved into an auto repair shop around 1908. Al ran the business until the late 1960s, with the business turned back into a bicycle sale and repair business as he aged.
COURTESY CHARLES FORSTER

OPPOSITE BOTTOM: Guiry Brothers Wallpaper store, circa 1920. Joe Guiry and his brothers opened their first paint and wallpaper store in Denver near Fifteenth Street and Court Place in 1899. The Guiry's bought and renovated many homes and built apartments in Denver. COURTESY PATTI REILLY CAPPS

ABOVE: Vegetable dealers in front of the Brule & Bourk Com. Co. at 1522 Market Street, circa 1920.
COURTESY DENVER PUBLIC LIBRARY, WESTERN HISTORY COLLECTION, ID# X-24078

ABOVE RIGHT: Proprietors August and Anna Jensen (in aprons) with their 17-year-old daughter Dagmar in their Capitol Hill Bakery located at 2216-2218 East Colfax Avenue, circa 1917. COURTESY JODIE RANKIN

RIGHT: Women working in the office of Daniels and Fisher, April 1917.
COURTESY KATHRYN HUG

OPPOSITE: John Epley, an employee of A. A. Vickers Petroleum Company, 1922. The gas station was on Speer Boulevard. COURTESY DIANA L. FREDERICK

ABOVE: Employees of the Lindquist Cracker Company at 512 Walnut Street in the Five Points neighborhood of Denver, 1921. COURTESY JEANNIE MCDONNELL

RIGHT: Office of John F. Mueller Investments, 1810 Stout Street, circa 1920. COURTESY CATHERINE MUELLER

OPPOSITE BOTTOM: Eighth Annual Convention of Association of Colored Railway Trainmen, July 20-26, 1925. COURTESY BLACK AMERICAN WEST MUSEUM, PAUL W. STEWART COLLECTION

LEFT: A group of Goodwill employees collect donations along Lawrence and Thirty-First Streets in the 1920s with the request, "Throw all your shoes at us!" COURTESY JESSICA HUDGINS SMITH, GOODWILL INDUSTRIES OF DENVER

BELOW LEFT: The Denver Powerine Company tanker truck at 3604 Fox Street, circa 1925. COURTESY BEN CABRAL

OPPOSITE: Golden Eagle Dry Goods store delivery trucks and drivers, 1920s. It was a successful department store at Lawrence and Sixteenth Streets and was started by Leopold H. Guldman, a young businessman who came to the United States from Bavaria. COURTESY DAVID AND PAM WOLF

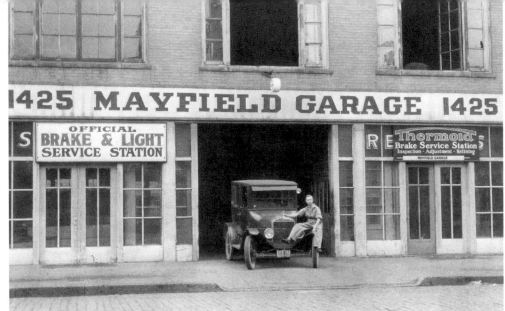

ABOVE: Employees and Nicholas Saraceno at his shoe shop on Nineteenth Avenue, April 1929. COURTESY JULIE SARACENO BOYD

ABOVE RIGHT: Mayfield Garage, 1425 Market Street, circa 1929. Ted Fitzgerald is on the fender of the car. The proprietor was W. J. Honeyman. COURTESY DUANE H. DUFF JR.

RIGHT: Capitol Shine & Hat Parlor on Fifteenth Street, circa 1927. The shop was owned by brothers Louis and Mike Georgopulos who came from Greece via Ellis Island in 1906. COURTESY BARRY GEORGOPULOS

OPPOSITE: Factory workers inside DeLine Box Company at Eleventh and Santa Fe, 1920s. COURTESY MILE HIGH PHOTO, EUGENE B. RICE II

ABOVE: Employees of Chicago Burlington & Quincy Railroad (CB&Q) locomotive shops at Fifty-First and Bannock Streets, December 14, 1928. COURTESY MARVIN ALMQUIST

LEFT: Peck and Hills Furniture on Wynkoop Street, August 1928. From left: Henry Hunterman, Sy Scarry, unidentified, Warth La Crone, next four unidentified, Ed Priest, Harold Westcot, Sam Wilson, unidentified, Bill Priest, Virgil Seely. COURTESY LORI BRONES ROBERTS

ABOVE: Four-booth beauty shop, cleaning and pressing shop, and a tailor shop inside the Arcade Mini-Mall, circa 1935. Second from left is Charles R. Cousins Jr. Fourth from left is Delores Cousins.
COURTESY BLACK AMERICAN WEST MUSEUM, PAUL W. STEWART COLLECTION

ABOVE LEFT: Drug store inside the Arcade Mini-Mall, owned and operated by Charles and Alta Cousins at 725 East Twenty-Sixth Avenue, circa 1935. At far left is Delores Cousins. The child seated at far right is Craig R. Cousins. Owner Charles L. Cousins is third from the right. Dr. Trimble, the pharmacist, is second from the right and soda fountain manager, Ted Collins, is at far right.
COURTESY BLACK AMERICAN WEST MUSEUM, PAUL W. STEWART COLLECTION

LEFT: Barber shop inside the Arcade Mini-Mall, owned by Charles L. Cousins, circa 1935. The little boy is identified as James Biffle.
COURTESY BLACK AMERICAN WEST MUSEUM, PAUL W. STEWART COLLECTION

OPPOSITE: Greenwald's Soda Fountain in the 1930s. Working behind the counter (third from the right) is Ruth Mosco who worked here in her high school years. She married her high school sweetheart, Elliot Handler, and would go on to found the largest toy company in the world, Mattel.
COURTESY DENVER PUBLIC LIBRARY, WESTERN HISTORY COLLECTION, ID# X-24098

HARRY'S
MOTOR CYCLE
SERVICE

SUPER X HILL CLIMB CHAMPION

HARRY'S
MOTOR CYCLE
SERVICE

LEFT: Offices of American Woodmen's Life Insurance Company, located at 2130 Downing Street, circa 1935. It was said to be the only company in Denver that would hire qualified young black women in secretarial positions. COURTESY BLACK AMERICAN WEST MUSEUM, PAUL W. STEWART COLLECTION

OPPOSITE TOP: Armour & Company packing house employees, January 25, 1929. An image of the company's office staff is inset at top center. COURTESY ERLINDA ARCHULETA

OPPOSITE BOTTOM: Harry Tagaris (right) was the owner of Harry's Motorcycle Service, 1930. The man on the left is believed to have loaned money to Harry so he could start the business. His name is not known. COURTESY HARRY J. TAGARIS

BELOW: David Sturgeon (far left) and his fleet of cars from Sturgeon Electric Company, 1929. Sturgeon Electric Company, Inc. (Sturgeon Electric) was founded in Denver by David Dwight "DD" Sturgeon in 1912. Mr. Sturgeon was an active member of the Denver community, and was instrumental in the development of the industry, downtown Denver and in the growth of the city. In 2012, Sturgeon Electric celebrated 100 years in business as a leading regional specialty contractor serving the electrical needs of customers throughout Arizona, Colorado and Utah. COURTESY JAMES F. KIMSEY

ABOVE LEFT: "Fritz," son of C. F. and Josephine Maler, loading potted plants for shipment at 3914 West Twenty-Ninth Avenue, circa 1930. This early 1930s White truck was used to transport potted plants from the greenhouse to the shipping department of C. F. Maler Florist. COURTESY J. F. MALER

BELOW LEFT: Joe Vendegina (right) peddling vegetables and fruit in North Denver, July 21, 1936. Italian street vendors were known by the color of their trucks; Vendegina's truck was bright green. He picked up fresh produce daily from the Denargo Market during the spring and summer months. He loved to hand out slices of watermelon to the neighborhood kids on a hot summer day. Vendegina purchased the truck with cash on March 6, 1936, from the James Motor Company in Denver. A local craftsman named Niederhaut adapted the box from a horse-drawn wagon to the 1936 Dodge chassis and built the canopy over it to shield the produce from the sun. Vendegina sold produce in the area from this truck for 28 years. COURTESY BYRNE AND VENDEGINA FAMILIES (SUBMITTED BY CINDY BYRNE BALL)

OPPOSITE TOP LEFT: Workers at Gardner Denver at Thirty-Ninth and Williams Streets in the late 1930s. The company was founded by Robert W. Gardner in 1859. COURTESY KAREN PALEN

OPPOSITE BOTTOM LEFT: New signage at the Gem Theatre on Curtis Street in the 1930s, courtesy of Gordon Sign. COURTESY GORDON SIGN

OPPOSITE TOP RIGHT: Interior of the umbrella shop owned by Elsie and William Capella, 515 Fifteenth Street, 1935. COURTESY JEAN ALSOP

OPPOSITE BOTTOM RIGHT: The Smith Restaurant at the National Western Stock Show in 1936. Jeanette Smith Walsh, daughter of S. C. Smith, is in the foreground. COURTESY FRANCIS & DONNA WALSH (WALSH/SMITH FAMILY PHOTOS)

ABOVE: The owners and employees of Goldberg Brothers Hardware & Tinner's Supplies outside their Denver headquarters, July 18, 1939. COURTESY GOLDBERG BROTHERS, INC.

RIGHT: Dorothy Mittag Robertson and her panel delivery truck for Santa Fe Floral shop, which she owned and operated at 865 Santa Fe Drive, 1937. COURTESY MARILYN ROBERTSON

FAR RIGHT: Tom Carroll Jr., son of Thomas Carroll, owner of the Carroll Dairy, standing in front of the creamery at 24 East Alameda Avenue, circa 1937.
COURTESY JUDY CARROLL BLACKFORD

OPPOSITE: Budweiser Clydesdales on Welton Street in front of Lincoln Liquors in 1937. The store was owned by Jack, Abe, and Harry Weinstock. Harry and Jack are left and second from left, respectively, in the group of four men in front of the horses.
COURTESY HONEY GOLDBERG

CHAPTER FIVE

COMMUNITY

Nothing reflects the spirit of community within a city or county like its people, and Denver is certainly no different. Our pioneers had to be strong to settle this new land with few resources and a sometimes hostile environment.

But as churches and neighborhoods began to replace the rural, agrarian existence, people could turn to their community for support and help. Churches became a centerpiece of collaboration and socialization among the congregants.

Churches also spurred volunteerism in many forms. In 1905, the Evangelical Lutheran Sanitarium Association purchased 20 acres for a health farm to treat tuberculosis. Volunteers of America established Fresh Air Camp on Lookout Mountain to serve low-income children.

The United Way, founded in Denver in 1887, has become an internationally recognized philanthropic organization.

This chapter shows the faces of hard-working people and people at their best: Christmas, weddings, formal family portraits posed with their most-prized possessions—their homes and cars.

You will see the faces of minorities who struggled to make a living in a segregated world. There was the famous Dr. Justina Ford who delivered 7,000 babies to women who had been turned away from Denver hospitals. Dr. Thomas Ernest McClain brought needed dental health to the Five Points neighborhood. William Daniels Fountain became a veterinarian and worked for the US Department of Agriculture. The William Chin family played a leading role in Denver's Chinatown.

OPPOSITE: Members of the Denver Lions Club erect a sign near the city limits in 1939. COURTESY DENVER LIONS CLUB

ABOVE: Brothers Henry and Walter Hansen, circa 1895. COURTESY MARJORIE HOOK

ABOVE LEFT: Tent colony health farm for the treatment of tuberculosis at West Thirty-Eighth Avenue and Wadsworth Boulevard, winter of 1905. The newly founded Evangelical Lutheran Sanitarium Association purchased 20 acres for the health farm in May 1905. COURTESY HATTIE A. POST

LEFT: John J. Epley home at 1939 West Howard, 1890. Sitting in front: Theressa Smith, L. E. Epley, May Ray, Mina Wallace. Standing: Perry Hinds, Minnie Epley, John Hinds, A. E. Epley. COURTESY DIANA L. FREDERICK

OPPOSITE: Esther (8), Willie (10), and Marie (12) with their baby brother Charles Howard, celebrating Christmas at 3433 Williams Street in the Whittier District of Denver, 1911. COURTESY KARIN CONWAY

ABOVE: Convention of the Midland Club and Western Confectionery Association, July 13-15, 1920. COURTESY EUGENE B. RICE II

RIGHT: Maclovia Gonzales and Tiofilo Gallegos wedding photo, 1920. COURTESY SANDRA SMITH

OPPOSITE BOTTOM LEFT: Wedding party for John Joling and Evelyn (Henricks) Joling, likely at the boarding house at 1700 South Broadway run by Evelyn and her mother, May 27, 1917. Evelyn is third from the left in the back row and John is on her left. COURTESY JUDY KISSINGER

OPPOSITE BOTTOM RIGHT: William Daniels Fountain, a doctor of veterinary medicine, June 1917. Through promotions over a 42-year period, he became supervisor of veterinarians at the Denver stockyards and also worked in the consumer and marketing division for the USDA.
COURTESY BLACK AMERICAN WEST MUSEUM, PAUL W. STEWART COLLECTION

ABOVE: Wedding party of Margareta A. Fischer "Reta" and Fredrick William "Bill" Rehkow Jr., August 15, 1926. COURTESY JERRY REHKOW

ABOVE LEFT: Kraut family photograph, 1925. From left: Rose, Nathan, Reba, Dorothy, Harold (front). COURTESY MINDY KRAUT

BELOW LEFT: Dr. Justina Ford, circa 1920s. The first African-American female doctor in Denver, Ford was initially denied a medical license. She and her patients were also denied access to Denver hospitals. Even so, late in life she estimated that she had delivered roughly 7,000 babies during her 50-year career. In 1984, her Arapaho Street house and home office, scheduled for demolition by the city, was moved to its current location on California Street where it serves as the home of the Black American West Museum and Heritage Center. COURTESY BLACK AMERICAN WEST MUSEUM, PAUL W. STEWART COLLECTION

OPPOSITE: William and Daisy Chin and family, circa 1928. Standing in front, from left, are twins Helen Chin Lum and Henry Chin. Seated: William C. Chin, Daisy Y. Chin, William L. Chin, Edward L. Chin. Back row: Wawa Chin Jew, Frances Chin Wong, Hazel Chin Hong. William L. Chin was born in Black Hawk in 1888 and passed away in October 1939. He was known as the "Mayor of Denver's Chinatown." He married Daisy on November 9, 1909. William's father was Chin Lin Sou, memorialized in stained glass at the Colorado State Capitol. Chin Lin Sou managed the Chinese Laborers who built the Pacific Railroad. William and Daisy are survived by their families who are six generations strong. COURTESY CAROLYN G. KUHN

CHAPTER SIX

RECREATION AND ENTERTAINMENT

Denverites worked hard and played hard. From organized sports to clubs and organizations, from theater and music to amusement parks, there was something for everyone.

The Denver Athletic Club's football team drew large crowds, as did company-sponsored teams such as the Nickel in Slot baseball team (Colorado Telephone employees), Cottrells' men's semi-pro baseball, Bayly-Underhill Manufacturing Company men's and women's baseball teams, and Foreman's National Detective Agency amateur basketball. But if team sports weren't your fancy, there were also car races and horse races.

City parks offered a cooling-off spot on lazy, warm summer days. City Lake Park was a very popular spot in the early 1900s, as was Civic Center park. Amusement parks such as Elitch Gardens and White City, which featured more than 100,000 electric lights and later became Lakeside Amusement

Park, offered a more thrilling experience.

Clubs and organizations offered lower-key entertainment venues. Some, including the United Spanish Society, supported ethnic traditions and customs. Others were more focused on fun and exercise, such as the Denver Wheel Club, which drew hundreds of cyclists.

The Denver nightlife was a vibrant scene with the renowned Theater Row, established in 1918, on Curtis Street. The street was sometimes called the "Great White Way" as a nod to its unprecedented use of electric lights.

The area was filled with people enjoying live stage and comedy shows, vaudeville acts, movies, and dinner theater. There were places that specialized in all forms of music: symphonic, jazz, opera, dance, big band, and "race music."

OPPOSITE: Driver Roy Sherman with car owner and builder Vic Felt at the Speaks Powerine station at Eighth and Lincoln Streets, circa 1939. Sherman was the 1939 Colorado high point driver in this D. O. Hal powered midget. COURTESY LEROY BYERS

ABOVE: *The Denver Post*-sponsored Sells Floto Circus traveled the continent with Bonfils, the smiling hippo, one of the best-known attractions in the circus business. Pictured with Bonfils is Effie Rairden (left) and Madge England, circa 1927.
COURTESY THE DENVER POST ARCHIVES

LEFT: The Tabor Grand Opera House on Curtis Street, 1935. Horace A. W. Tabor, having made his fortune in the silver mines of Leadville, and having already built a great opera house, built this one in 1881 to impress his soon-to-be second wife, Baby Doe. It opened with Emma Abbott singing "Lucia." The old Sixteenth Street Post Office and Custom House can be seen at the right.
COURTESY SALLIE C. LEWIS

OPPOSITE: Pete Smythe's Orchestra, featuring vocalist Miss Mary Elizabeth Bailey, at the Cosmopolitan Hotel's Silver Glade ballroom at Eighteenth Avenue and Broadway, circa 1934. Pete Smythe is in the white suit and Bailey is to his right. H. R. "Pete" Wall is fourth from the left, W. C. "Kayo" Lam is third from the right and Elwood Kullgren is at far right. The Silver Glade ballroom was billed as "The Coolest Place in Denver," in part because it was air-conditioned.
COURTESY GEORGE FILMER (MARY ELIZABETH BAILEY'S SON) AND PETE WALL (H. R. "PETE" WALL'S SON)

ABOVE: Hattie McDaniel (standing, center right), the first African-American to win an Oscar in 1940 for her supporting role as Mammy in *Gone with the Wind*, performed with the George Morrison Orchestra in the 1920s. While attending Denver's East High School in the early 1900s, McDaniel started professionally singing, dancing and performing skits in shows as part of her family's vaudeville act, The Mighty Minstrels. She dropped out of high school in 1909 to focus on her singing and dancing. The George Morrison Orchestra sometimes played at the Albany Hotel, which had not previously allowed performances by African-American musical groups. Photo circa 1928. COURTESY BLACK AMERICAN WEST MUSEUM, PAUL W. STEWART COLLECTION

ABOVE LEFT: Foreman's National Detective Agency amateur basketball team, 1931. COURTESY FRED STRELTZER

LEFT: George Morrison (seated on piano stool at left) studied classical violin in Boulder and Denver before refining his skills under the tutelage of Fritz Kreisler in Chicago. Unable to perform with any symphony orchestra, he started his own orchestra in Denver. The group recorded "race records" (early jazz) for Columbia Records in 1920. They toured Europe where they played a command performance for the King and Queen of England. The pianist was Mary Byrd, wife of saxophonist Cuthbert Byrd. Photo circa 1920. COURTESY BLACK AMERICAN WEST MUSEUM, PAUL W. STEWART COLLECTION

OPPOSITE: Noble Sissle and his international orchestra at Elitch Gardens in 1937. Denver vocalist and dancer Delno Polk Bailey is standing, fifth from the left. COURTESY BLACK AMERICAN WEST MUSEUM, PAUL W. STEWART COLLECTION

ABOVE: Ice skating in City Park, circa 1939. COURTESY DENVER PUBLIC LIBRARY, WESTERN HISTORY COLLECTION, ID# CPHOTO422

RIGHT: Aerial view of Wellshire Municipal Golf Course, July 11, 1939. COURTESY JIM LEIGHTON

OPPOSITE: The State Theater, 1630 Curtis Street, in its heyday, 1935. The theater opened in 1914 as the Strand. It was extensively modernized and reopened in 1925 as the State and was torn down circa 1951. COURTESY SALLIE C. LEWIS

CHAPTER SEVEN

PUBLIC SERVICE

Communities cannot thrive without the sacrifice of public servants who dedicate their lives to making them a better place for its residents. From its politicians, sheriffs and policemen, postal workers, and doctors and nurses, Denver benefited from their efforts.

Early fire departments relied on volunteers and horse-drawn equipment and would not see motorized vehicles until 1917. When considering the early use of wooden structures, the efforts of the fire brigades were greatly valued.

The sheriffs and police departments had their hands full taming this Wild West settlement into the "Queen City of the Plains." Early modes of patrolling were from horseback and horse-drawn carriages, but officers quickly adopted automobiles, trucks, motorcycles, and even airplanes to cover the expanding county.

In 1926, Lowry Field's first buildings were erected at East Thirty-Eighth Avenue and Dahlia Street but didn't really take hold until facilities were moved in 1937 to East Sixth Avenue and Quebec Street, on Denver's east side. Soon, Lowry became a hub to train Air Force personnel. The area grew to become almost a city of its own, fully independent of the day-to-day operations of the city of Denver.

OPPOSITE: Denver Fire Department Chief Healy standing with the new Engine No. 2 and crew at Fire Station No. 1 at 1326 Tremont Place in downtown Denver, circa 1925. COURTESY DENVER PUBLIC LIBRARY, WESTERN HISTORY COLLECTION, ID# X-29582

ABOVE: A large crowd gathers to hear President Theodore Roosevelt speak in 1903. COURTESY DALE C. BEHSE

RIGHT: President Theodore Roosevelt addressing a large Denver crowd in 1903. He is standing on a chair and spoke without any kind of loudspeakers or public address system. COURTESY DALE C. BEHSE

OPPOSITE: Denver Woodie Fisher No. 1 on Lawrence Street, between Fifteenth and Sixteenth Streets, circa 1876. This was the city's first hose company. The city installed its first fire hydrants a few years earlier.
COURTESY DENVER FIREFIGHTERS MUSEUM

ABOVE RIGHT: Denver Policeman Walter Alexander Osborn walked the beat on Larimer Street in the early 1900s. He retired in 1918. COURTESY RUTH BRICKLEY

ABOVE MIDDLE: The United States Post Office (later the Customs House) at Sixteenth and Arapahoe Streets, circa 1888.
COURTESY DENVER PUBLIC LIBRARY, WESTERN HISTORY COLLECTION, ID# WHJ-1573

ABOVE LEFT: Martin J. Casey, a veteran of the Denver Police Department for more than 30 years (1877-1909), wearing his captain's uniform and badge, circa 1907. Casey immigrated to the United States from Ireland sometime prior to 1865, moved from Pennsylvania to Colorado in 1874, and settled in Denver by 1877. COURTESY MARY ANN CASEY

LEFT: Denver Fire Department firemen harnessing horses to a ladder truck, circa 1900. COURTESY ROBERT GRAEBER

OPPOSITE: Steamer No. 1 Station at the corner of W. Colfax Ave. and Broadway (site of the present Pioneer Monument), circa 1889.
COURTESY DENVER FIREFIGHTERS MUSEUM

ABOVE: Denver Police Officer William Goldblatt (left) and his family in front of their home at Fourteenth and Newton Streets, circa 1914. William's wife, Helen, is at right. Their children (from left) are Marvin and Ruth. COURTESY HELENE HOFFMAN

ABOVE RIGHT: Members of the Denver Police Department, circa 1915. COURTESY HELENE HOFFMAN

RIGHT: Firemen with horse-drawn wagons and a motorized chief's car at Fire Engine House No. 11, 301 Cherokee Street, circa 1909. The two-story brick building was in use from 1890 until 1937. COURTESY ROBERT GRAEBER

OPPOSITE: Hose Station No. 1 at 600 South Broadway, circa 1894. The photo was taken soon after South Denver was annexed to Denver in 1894. The station was originally South Denver Russell Hose No. 1, when it was a volunteer station. The station still exists. COURTESY DENVER FIREFIGHTERS MUSEUM

ABOVE: Denver Fire Department Truck Company No. 4 (Station 8) at City Hall station (Station 6), circa 1917. This was the department's first motorized ladder truck.
COURTESY DENVER FIREFIGHTERS MUSEUM

LEFT: Station No. 8, Sixteenth and Marion Streets, circa 1917. In front of the station are the first motorized pumper (left) purchased in 1915, and the first complete motorized ladder truck, purchased in 1917.
COURTESY DENVER FIREFIGHTERS MUSEUM

OPPOSITE: A group of Denver Police officers with bushel baskets of food, doing charitable work, circa 1915.
COURTESY DENVER PUBLIC LIBRARY, WESTERN HISTORY COLLECTION, ID# X-29670

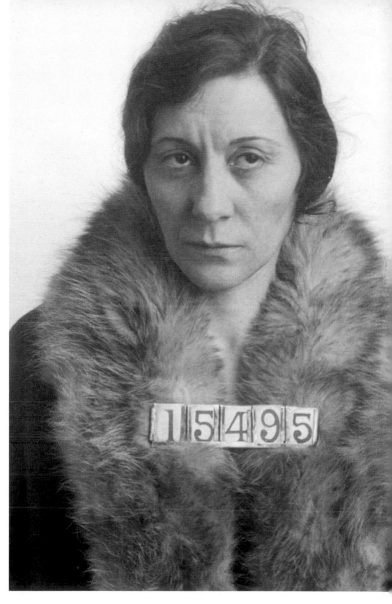

ABOVE LEFT: Denver Fire Department original Station No. 3 at Glenarm Place and North Washington Street, circa 1920s. The station still exists and was the home of the first Denver Fire Department African-American Engine Company. COURTESY DENVER FIREFIGHTERS MUSEUM

ABOVE RIGHT: Farice King, arrested for the murder of Denver police officer Robert K. Evans in November 1928. King was a nurse at Denver General Hospital where officer Evans was recovering from a gunshot wound suffered days earlier in the line of duty. She also happened to be a jilted former mistress of Evans. On November 29, 1928, King purchased a $6 revolver at a pawn shop on Larimer Street, walked into Evans' hospital room and shot him twice at close range as he slept. COURTESY COLORADO STATE ARCHIVES

OPPOSITE: Firemen in fire trucks on the Market Street Bridge in front of the City Hall Fire Station No. 6, circa 1924. COURTESY DENVER PUBLIC LIBRARY, WESTERN HISTORY COLLECTION, ID# X-29558

ABOVE: Denver Branch 47, National Association of Letter Carriers, in front of the post office in downtown Denver, September 26, 1926. COURTESY CHARLENE PORTER

RIGHT: The Colorado State Capitol building reflected in the Civic Center Park pool, circa 1930s. COURTESY MARION LEE EPPERSON

OPPOSITE BOTTOM: Colorado Sheriffs and Peace Officers' Association members in front of the Brown Palace, January 1934. COURTESY TODD AND RENEE HOPKLINS

ABOVE: Tent City, north of Sixth Avenue on Lowry Field, is ready for 200 students to move in, July 1939. COURTESY WINGS OVER THE ROCKIES AIR & SPACE MUSEUM

ABOVE LEFT: Construction of Hangar No. 1 at Lowry Field, circa 1939. COURTESY WINGS OVER THE ROCKIES AIR & SPACE MUSEUM

LEFT: Traffic officer C. Quintan giving a ticket, circa 1927. COURTESY DENVER POLICE MUSEUM

OPPOSITE: Traffic duty in the early 1930s before the three-wheelers were introduced in 1933. COURTESY DENVER POLICE MUSEUM

CHAPTER EIGHT

CELEBRATIONS

Everyone loves a parade, and Denver really knew how to throw one! There were parades organized to honor the men going off to war—including the Spanish-American War and World War I—as well as to celebrate the end of WWI. Civil servants and service organizations, including the Elks Club and the sanitation street-cleaning department, took to the streets to show their pride.

There were parades to celebrate the holidays such as the Fourth of July, Mexico's Independence Day, and other events to promote political activities.

Denver residents came out in droves to see visiting dignitaries such as President Theodore Roosevelt, Queen Marie of Romania, and Charles Lindbergh.

And what is not to love about the Festival of Mountain and Plain, and the Puritan Maid Pie-Eating Contest?

OPPOSITE: Employees of the City of Denver drive truck and horse-drawn wagons with water tanks in the Denver Police and Firemen's Parade on Seventeenth Street, May 1921. COURTESY DENVER PUBLIC LIBRARY, WESTERN HISTORY COLLECTION, ID# X-23765

ABOVE: Julie Kaub, Lona Fisher, and Emmie Bloedorn (seated), won a special prize at a carnival during the Festival of Mountain and Plain, 1896. This was an annual celebration of pioneer days in the Old West held in early October in Denver from 1895 to 1899, and in 1901 with a final attempt at revival in 1912. COURTESY MARILYN KAUB

ABOVE RIGHT: Zang Bros. Co. float in the Festival of Mountain and Plain, circa 1896. The festival was the idea of civic leaders to lift the spirits of Colorado residents in the wake of an economic downturn linked to the plummeting price of silver.
COURTESY DENVER PUBLIC LIBRARY, WESTERN HISTORY COLLECTION, ID# X-25028

RIGHT: Colonel Irving Hale marches his troops, the First Colorado Infantry, down Sixteenth Street during the Spanish American War. Officers on horseback and troops parade by the Golden Eagle Dry Goods store and crowds of onlookers. COURTESY DENVER PUBLIC LIBRARY, WESTERN HISTORY COLLECTION, ID# Z-3006

OPPOSITE: Hook and Ladder Company No. 1 passing by city hall during a parade, circa 1912. COURTESY DENVER FIREFIGHTERS MUSEUM

ABOVE: Champa Street between Fourteenth and Fifteenth during the 1908 Democratic National Convention. Wagons carry snow and signs that read "From Summer's Glow To Winter's Snow - From the Moffat Road." COURTESY DENVER PUBLIC LIBRARY, WESTERN HISTORY COLLECTION, ID# Z-1014

RIGHT: An unidentified group in an automobile decorated for a Fourth of July Parade, circa 1915.
COURTESY CHARLOTTE A. WINZENBURG

LEFT: President Theodore Roosevelt riding in a carriage through Denver on his visit on August 29, 1910, as an entourage of men follow the carriage. COURTESY DENVER PUBLIC LIBRARY, WESTERN HISTORY COLLECTION, ID# RH-232

ABOVE: World War I parade, circa 1917.
COURTESY DARCIE MEIERBACHTOL

ABOVE LEFT: Elevated view of an Elks Club Parade with uniformed marchers on Seventeenth Street, circa 1915. Buntings and banners decorate the street lamps and the Brown Palace Hotel.
COURTESY DENVER PUBLIC LIBRARY, WESTERN HISTORY COLLECTION, ID# RH-714

LEFT: Denver Sanitation Street Cleaning Department participating in a parade passing through the intersection of Broadway and Sixteenth Streets, circa 1910. COURTESY DENVER PUBLIC LIBRARY, WESTERN HISTORY COLLECTION, ID# X-23670

OPPOSITE: Jubilant Denverites celebrate the end of World War I along Sixteenth Street at the intersection of Champa Street. COURTESY DENVER PUBLIC LIBRARY, WESTERN HISTORY COLLECTION, ID# Z-83

ABOVE: Members of the International Church of the Foursquare Gospel, founded by Evangelist Aimee Semple McPherson, parade south on Broadway, August 1937. COURTESY DENVER PUBLIC LIBRARY, WESTERN HISTORY COLLECTION, ID# Z-136

TOP: A large crowd gathers on Tenth Street in front of Tivoli-Union Brewery to celebrate Mexico's independence, September 16, 1928.
COURTESY ARLENE AND WILLIAM MACKINTOSH

LEFT: Four hundred men and students from the training camp at Fort Logan, parade down Sixteenth Street in 1921 before attending the circus as guests of *The Denver Post.* COURTESY THE DENVER POST ARCHIVES

OPPOSITE: People cheering from bleachers at Denver University stadium as Charles Lindbergh passes by in an automobile in 1927. He landed at Lowry Field to visit Denver after recently completing his solo flight across the Atlantic Ocean.
COURTESY DENVER PUBLIC LIBRARY, WESTERN HISTORY COLLECTION, ID# RH-480